The Mental Health Survival Guide

(Because It's A Jungle Out There)

An Swinnen

The Mental Health Survival Guide

(Because It's A Jungle Out There)

Copyright © 2020 An Swinnen. All Rights Reserved.

The use of any part of this publication reproduced, transmitted in any form or by any means, electronic, mechanical, recording or otherwise, or stored in a retrieval system, without the prior written permission of the publisher is an infringement of the copyright law. Any request for photocopying, recording, or for storing of information and retrieval systems of any art of this book should be directed in writing to info@becsltd.com

The information given in this book should not be treated as a substitute for professional medical advice. Individuals should always consult a medical practitioner. Any use of the information presented in this book is at the reader's discretion and risk. Neither the author nor the publishers can be held responsible for any loss, claim or damage arising out of the use, or misuse, of the suggestions made, the failure to take medical advice or for any material on third party websites.

Proofread by Dr Bridget Andrews

Cover Design by Ian Doughty

Cartoons by depositphotos

ISBN: 978-0-9567007-2-8

Published by Business English Consulting Service Ltd

126 Aldersgate Street, London EC1A 4JQ

To everyone who made it possible for me to write this book

About the Author

An Swinnen is the Managing Director of BECS which she founded in 2004. BECS is an award-winning training company based in London which specialises in business, management and mental health training and coaching worldwide.

In 2011 An was awarded the British Business Forum Excellence Certificate by Baroness Emma Nicholson of Winterbourne at the British Embassy in Kuwait. In 2013 An received the Venus Networker of the Year in Devon Award in the UK and in 2015 An was in the final of the UK Trainer of the Year Award in London.

An is the best-selling author of "The Business Survival Guide (Because It's A Jungle Out There)" which tells you what you really need to know to be a success in business.

An is not only a qualified teacher and training expert; she is also a Clinical Solution Focused Psychotherapist and author of "Brain Based Stress Management". She is a member of the National Board for Modern Psychotherapy.

Foreword

One in four people in the world will be affected by mental disorders at some point in their lives. Around 450 million people currently suffer from such conditions, placing mental disorders among the leading causes of ill-health and disability worldwide. Thankfully, despite some very stressful jobs, I have not suffered from mental health problems."

I always wondered why some are affected by stress more than others. The answer lies in science. When I studied the brain to become a solution focused psychotherapist, I realised that my healthy lifestyle and outlook on life played a big part.

My tips and advice are based on personal experience and research from many neurologists, psychologists, psychiatrists, universities and other organisations dedicated to understanding mental health and making us feel better. A special thank you goes to Dr Bridget Andrews for proofreading this book. Dr Andrews has an MSc in Foundations of Clinical Neuropsychology and a PhD in Cognitive Neuroscience.

The positive and inspiring message of this book is that you are in control of your mental health. Sit back, relax and enjoy the ride!

Contents

What is Stress?	13
Is Stress Dangerous?	15
The Brain	17
The Intellectual Brain	19
The Boss	21
The Daydreamer	23
The Primitive Brain	25
The Bodyguard	27
The Filing Cabinet	29
The Chemist	31
The Primitive Brain's Opt Out Clauses	33
Depression	35
Antidepressants	37
Anxiety	39
Anger	41
Your Stress Bucket	43
REM Sleep	45
Why Do We Sleep?	47
Sleeping Tips	49
Why Do We Dream?	51
Serotonin and Your Stress Bucket	53

Positive Action	55
Positive Interaction	57
Positive Thoughts	59
Other Serotonin Producers	61
Why am I Self-Destructive?	63
Exercise	65
Brain Food	67
Touch	69
Music	71
Nature	73
Meditation	75
Laughter	77
The Internet	79
Smoking	81
Drugs	83
Why Do Others Stress Me Out?	85
DISC Personality Types	87
The Dominant Type	89
The Influential Type	91
The Steady Type	93
The Compliant Type	95
Why Can't I Change?	97

Dealing With Big Changes and Loss	99
Mental Health Disorders	101
Burnout	103
Pain	105
Suicide	107
Happiness	109
Creating Better Relationships	111
Smile	113
Setting Goals	115
Visualisation	117
Gratitude	119
Take Control	121
Help!	123
Useful Websites	125
More about BECS	126
Contact Details	129

"Tough day or tough life?"

What is Stress?

1. Stress is your body's way of responding to any kind of demand or threat.

2. Stress is a normal part of life.

3. Stress keeps you focused and alert and can feel enjoyable.

4. Stress is necessary to achieve your goals.

5. Without stress we would not survive.

He was having his usual good time on Monday morning.

Is Stress Dangerous?

1. A certain level of stress is necessary to help you prepare for challenging tasks such as exams, job interviews and presentations so enjoy it.
2. Stress causes the increase of adrenalin, cortisol and testosterone so we can react appropriately when we are in danger. Stress keeps us alive and safe.
3. After the physical and real danger has gone, the level of stress hormones decreases quickly but if the danger was emotional, it takes a lot longer to go down. Take long, deep breaths as oxygen in the blood helps lower that level.
4. Long-term emotional stress can cause serious health problems and death.
5. If you experience high blood pressure, fatigue, depression, anxiety or heart disease, consult your doctor immediately.

"Did you bring me a brain with no baggage?"

The Brain

1. The brain is the key to your mental health.

2. You can manipulate your brain into thinking you are happy and healthy.

3. Tricking your brain into feeling content is fun, free and easy.

4. The brain is programmed to keep you alive and well.

5. Your brain is awesome and very flexible. Cherish it!

THIS IS PROBABLY THE MOST ASTUTE, MATURE NOVEL OF THE LAST HALF CENTURY THAT I'VE JUST FINISHED... ME WANT ICE CREAM.

The Intellectual Brain

1. It is the brain you know as you. It is your conscious part that interacts with the world.

2. Animals do not have an intellectual brain as they do not have a concept of the future.

3. The intellectual brain is generally very positive.

4. It is very creative and comes up with fantastic solutions, so relax; your brain is on the case.

5. The intellectual brain has two modes: the focused mode and the diffused mode where you are daydreaming. You switch between the two all day long. You cannot be in both at the same time. The diffused mode gives your brain a chance to relax.

"Let's try it without the parachute."

The Boss

1. The pre-frontal cortex, the boss, is the most important part of your intellectual brain.

2. It is programmed to achieve your goals in life.

3. The boss is in charge and can kick in, overruling your emotional, primitive mind (except when you are in real physical danger such as a fire).

4. The boss is very positive and knows what it is doing so trust it. It will come up with a good plan of action.

5. The boss is calm and in control. If you feel down, stop, breathe and let your rational boss take over. It is very powerful.

The Daydreamer

1. The default network mode, the daydreamer, is the other part of your intellectual brain.

2. If you feel you are not getting anywhere, stop what you are doing and give the boss a rest.

3. Take yourself away from the task and do something different: go for a walk, ring a friend, have a coffee, watch television.

4. While you do relaxing, enjoyable things, your brain is still looking for solutions without you realising. The daydream mode will produce AHA moments and answers.

5. The daydreamer lets you try out different solutions in the safety of your brain. It saves you from losing your job, upsetting your friend or getting beaten up.

"I don't know about you, but I'm tired of this hostile work environment!"

The Primitive Brain

1. The primitive brain keeps you alive and is doing a great job.

2. It is a very negative brain as it thinks everything and everyone is going to kill you.

3. It cannot distinguish between reality and imagination so do not watch a horror movie in the evening. Your brain will think it is in real danger and you will not sleep well.

4. The primitive brain is not creative or innovative. It refers to past patterns of behaviour and information already stored in the brain.

5. The primitive brain includes the amygdala (the bodyguard), hippocampus (the filing cabinet) and hypothalamus (the chemist).

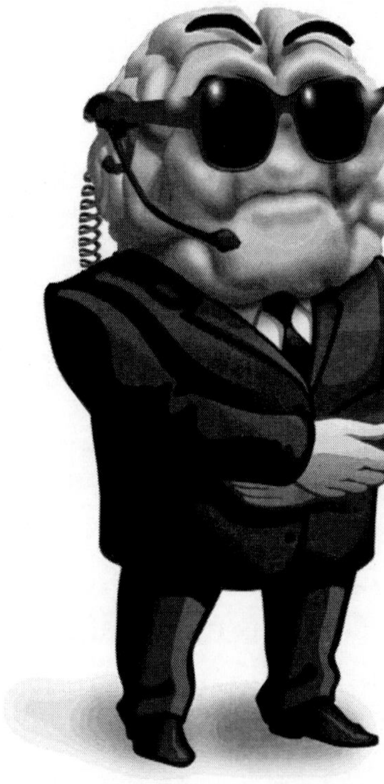

The Bodyguard

1. The amygdala in your primitive brain is your bodyguard.

2. The bodyguard protects you from physical and emotional threats.

3. The bodyguard is in constant communication with your filing cabinet and chemist to choose a reaction to threats: flight, fight or freeze.

4. The bodyguard is very protective and works around the clock to keep you safe.

5. It must be doing a great job if you are alive to read this book!

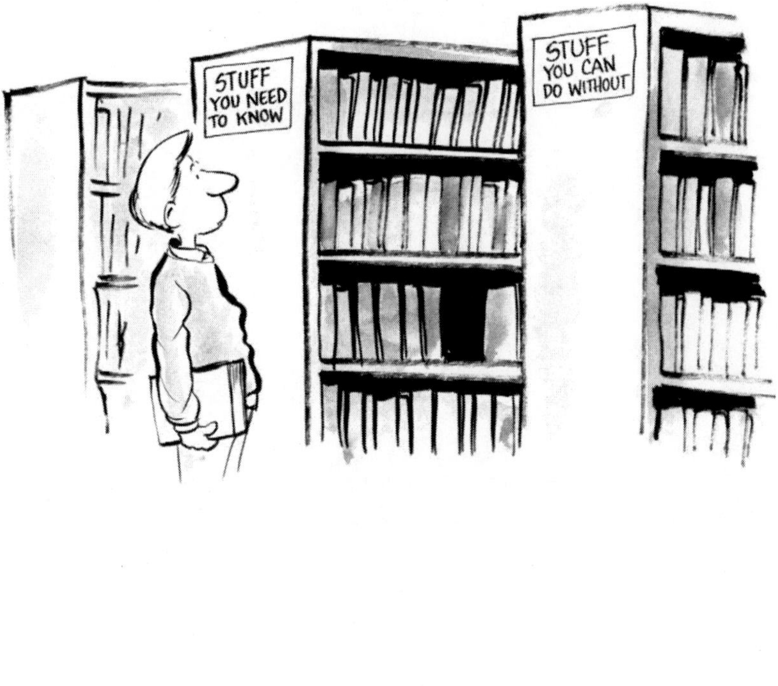
STUFF
YOU NEED
TO KNOW
STUFF
YOU CAN
DO WITHOUT

The Filing Cabinet

1. The hippocampus is the filing cabinet in your brain and records everything you have ever read, seen, smelled, heard and felt.

2. It records all information as the truth so be nice to people.

3. It tells your bodyguard whether a threat is real and what the best reaction would be, according what has been recorded in the past.

4. One way of manipulating your brain is to repeat very positive information about yourself so your filing cabinet records it as the truth. That will shape future decisions.

5. Be aware that your memory is not 100% reliable as films, books and dreams are also recorded as the truth.

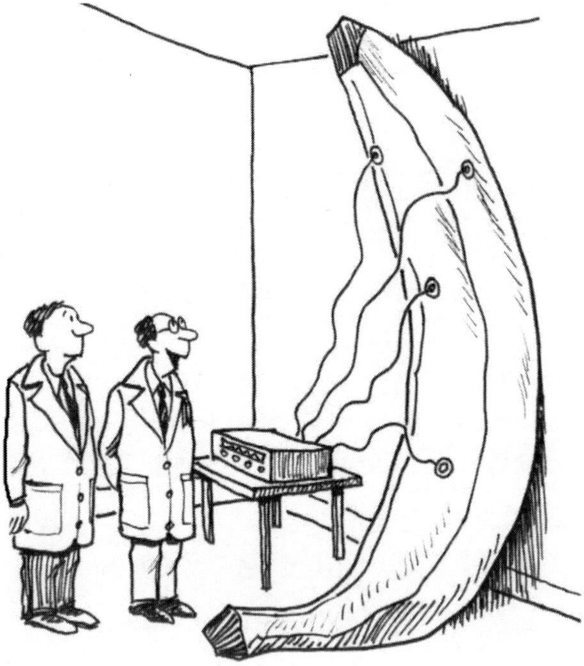

The Chemist

1. The hypothalamus, the chemist in your brain, regulates the chemical responses in your body and mind.

2. Your bodyguard sends the chemist messages that regulate your stress hormones.

3. Adrenalin, cortisol and testosterone make you stronger and enable you to run faster.

4. If you want to lower stress hormones, take deep breaths as more oxygen in your blood helps lower their levels.

5. Start thinking with your positive, rational and calm intellectual brain and feel better immediately.

"I'll only give you the paper if you promise not to let the news upset you."

The Primitive Brain's Opt Out Clauses

1. The primitive brain has three opt out clauses: depression, anxiety and anger.

2. The boss in your brain can overrule these opt out clauses so you feel happier and healthier.

3. Do not be a slave to depression, anxiety and anger.

4. You are in control! Switch from the primitive to the intellectual brain which is positive and rational.

5. Use the Swinnen Technique: take deep breaths, imagine your primitive brain being beaten by the intellectual brain, and smile.

"Wait, I'm YOUR therapist? I thought you were MY therapist."

Depression

1. If a caveman saw snow, floods or other tribes, he would stay in his cave until the danger had gone. His system would slow down to help him cope. The modern day symptoms of depression are the same.

2. Do not withdraw from life.

3. Be active. It will make you feel better.

4. Go out into nature and enjoy the weather.

5. Do not drink alcohol. It dehydrates your body and brain and you will feel worse after. Smoking also has negative consequences for your depression and health.

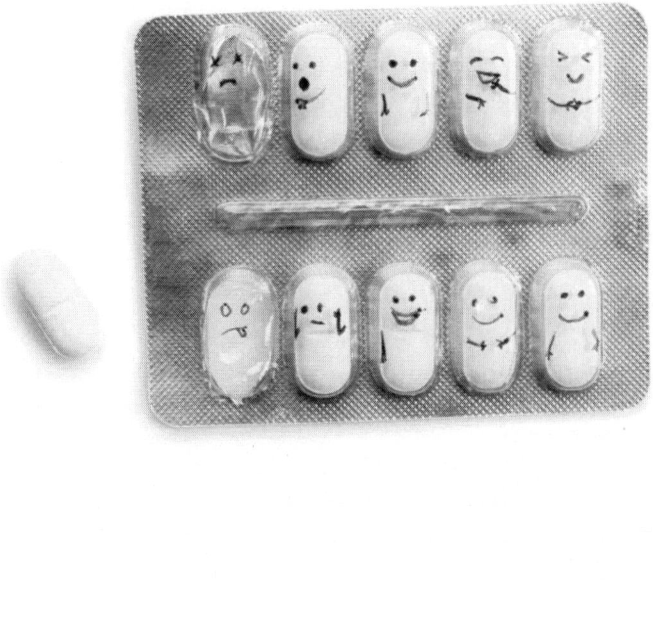

Antidepressants

1. Antidepressants are a type of medicine used to treat clinical depression. They can be used to treat a number of other conditions, including OCD and PTSD.

2. They help to artificially produce more serotonin and noradrenaline that regulate your general mood.

3. Antidepressants can make you feel better and treat some of the symptoms. They do not always address the causes.

4. They are usually used in combination with therapy to treat more severe depression.

5. Only doctors and psychiatrists can describe them for moderate and severe depression. They are not recommended for mild depression.

Anxiety

1. If the caveman was in the jungle with all its sounds and movements, his primitive brain would go into overdrive to deal with the dangers. Modern day symptoms of anxiety are the same.

2. Take deep breaths to reduce your stress hormones and you will feel better quickly.

3. Listen to relaxing and soothing music.

4. Let your intellectual brain take over and you will realise that your unpaid bills will not kill you.

5. Practice yoga and relax your body and mind. YouTube has thousands of excellent yoga lessons for all levels. It will allow you to take time out in the safety of your home.

"I could really use some aggressive skills."

Anger

1. Anger is a primitive way of increasing your strength to defend yourself.

2. Be careful! Adrenaline, cortisol and testosterone make you a lot stronger which means that fights can have fatal consequences.

3. Take deep breaths to decrease the stress hormone levels in your blood.

4. Walk away from the situation.

5. Let your intellectual brain take over and think of possible solutions.

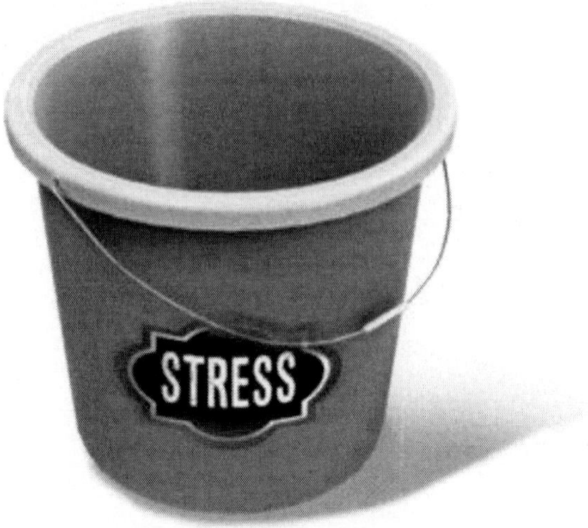
STRESS

Your Stress Bucket

1. Each person has a stress bucket in their brain.

2. During the day you put negative thoughts in your stress bucket and they turn into anxiety.

3. The negative thoughts can be about the past, the present or the future.

4. Stop thinking negatively because the filing cabinet in your brain cannot distinguish between reality and fiction. If you worry, your brain will think you are in real physical danger.

5. Make sure your stress bucket does not overflow for long periods as that can lead to depression and burnout.

"I read a story. Dr. Ehrlich is making rain sounds. Now why don't you just shut up and go to sleep?!"

REM Sleep

1. REM (Rapid Eye Movement) sleep empties your stress bucket at night.

2. During your REM sleep you re-run unresolved issues in clear or metaphorical (dreaming) language so you can deal with these during the night and then carry on with your life the next day.

3. Make sure you get the correct amount of REM sleep which is about 20% of your sleep.

4. The REM sleep comes in 4-6 cycles. To make sure you go through enough cycles, adults need about eight hours of sleep.

5. Do not sleep too much as REM sleep is very tiring.

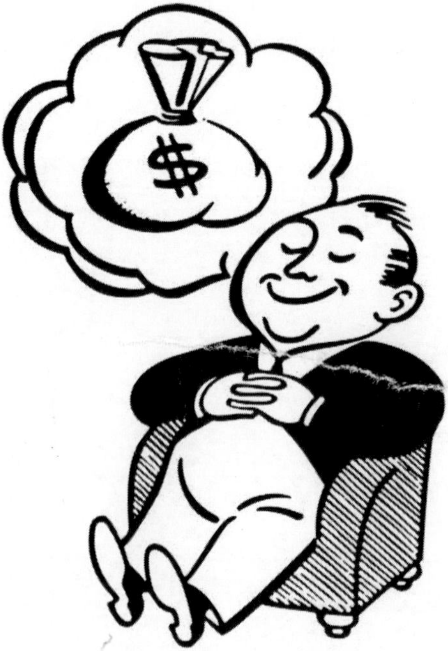

Why Do We Sleep?

1. Sleep is a complex process that is essential to the rejuvenation of the body and mind.

2. There are five stages of sleep and each serves a unique restorative function.

3. If you do not have enough sleep, you put your physical and mental health at risk.

4. If you have an important exam, job interview or presentation the next day, have an early night.

5. Adults should get eight hours of sleep and children a lot more, depending on their age. Learning, memorising and rationalising happens in our sleep.

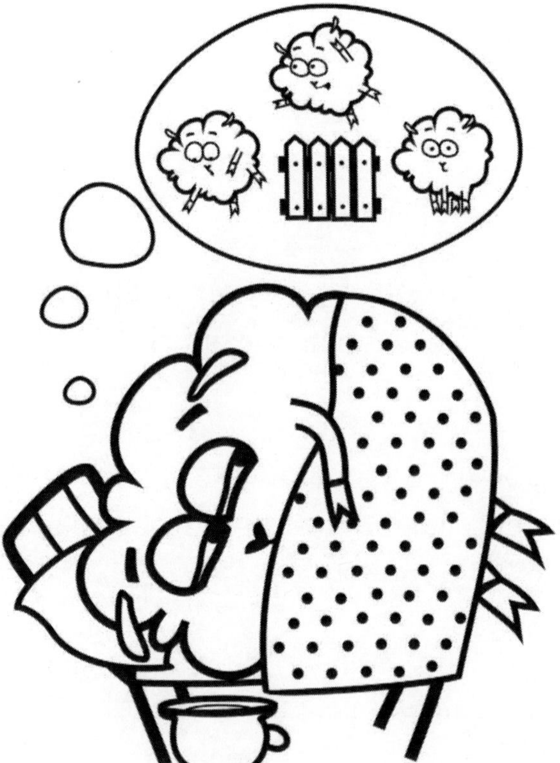

Why Can't I Sleep?

1. You have been piling too many negative thoughts into your stress bucket and sometimes it will overflow.

2. REM sleep is restricted to about 20% of your sleep patterns. If you go over, the mind will wake you up in the middle of the night. You feel wide awake and often feel quite miserable.

3. REM sleep is tiring. It requires enormous energy to diffuse the anxiety in your stress bucket. It exhausts you and makes you want to sleep even more during the day. That becomes a vicious circle.

4. Do not pile as many negative thoughts in your stress bucket.

5. Concentrate on the positive aspects of your life.

"As soon as she's out zap her with the brain probe!"

Sleeping Tips

1. Make sure your bedroom is very dark at night. The blue light of routers and TVs make your brain think it is daylight and will wake you up.

2. Make sure you have a good mattress. You should replace it every seven years.

3. Have a sleeping routine (very useful with children).

4. Listen to relaxing and calm music. Your body will synchronise with the beats of the music and your body and mind will slow down, ready to fall asleep.

5. Do a body scan when you are in bed. Tense each part of your body and let go so it is totally relaxed. Start with your head and move down to your toes.

"I think he's fake sleeping"

Why Do We Dream?

1. During REM sleep unfulfilled or unresolved emotions during the day are acted out in the form of metaphors in dreams.

2. You only dream about unresolved issues of that day. If you dream about something that happened a long time ago, it means that something triggered that memory.

3. Once you resolve the issue in your dream, e.g. you beat up your colleague, you can start the day afresh.

4. Do not make hasty decisions. Sleep on it.

5. Write down your dreams and try to analyse them.

"I still make this look good."

Serotonin

1. Serotonin is a neurotransmitter that regulates our general mood and appetite.

2. If you produce a constant flow of serotonin you feel happy and brave and you cope wonderfully.

3. When you produce enough serotonin, you do not fill up your stress bucket with negative thoughts.

4. If you are depressed, you produce a lot less serotonin. If you feel anxious, you produce too many stress hormones.

5. Alcohol stops the flow of serotonin by more than 75%, even after one drink. Nicotine halves the flow of serotonin so be aware.

No problem, thought Henry, I'll practice my putting.

Positive Actions

1. If you do things you like doing, you produce a steady flow of serotonin and you experience a general good mood.

2. When you enjoy what you do, you do not fill up your stress bucket as much.

3. Go for a walk, ring a friend, read your favourite magazine, watch football, go for a coffee, enjoy yourself!

4. Charity is a great way to feel happier.

5. Live in the moment and enjoy its beauty.

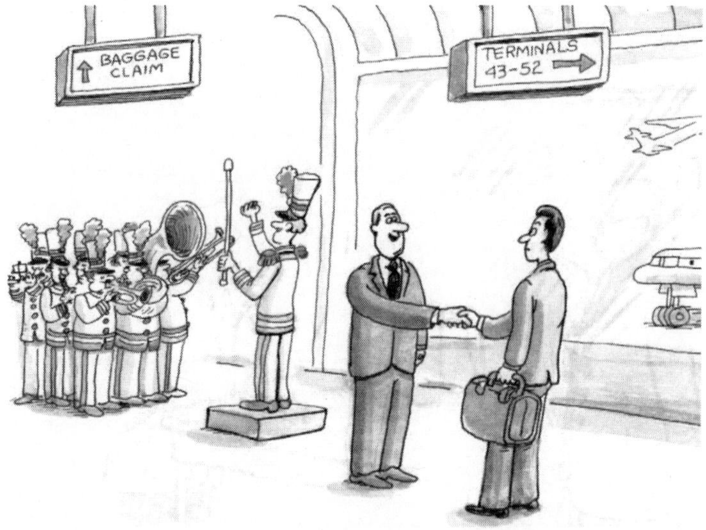
BAGGAGE CLAIM
TERMINALS 43-52

Positive Interactions

1. Positive interaction creates a steady flow of serotonin.

2. Be nice.

3. Say thank you to strangers who open doors, help you, stop for you at zebra crossings, etc.

4. Smile and others will smile back at you.

5. Let someone know you are thinking of them.

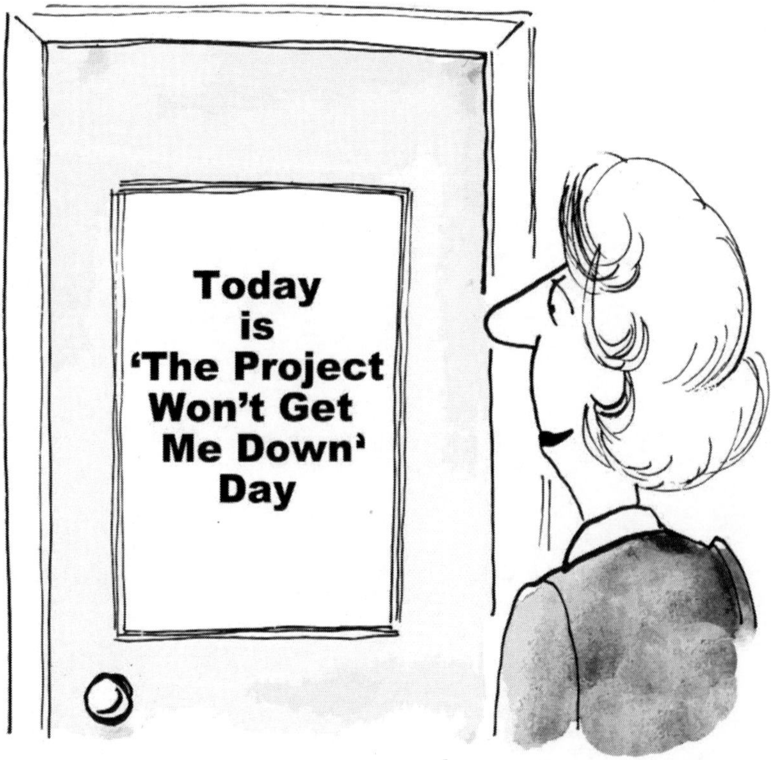
Today
is
‘The Project
Won’t Get
Me Down’
Day

Positive Thoughts

1. Positive thoughts produce a steady flow of serotonin.

2. If you think positive thoughts, you will not be filling up your stress bucket with negative ones.

3. If you start thinking negatively, stop and pause. It means your primitive brain has kicked in. Start thinking with your intellectual brain and you will be fine.

4. Surround yourself with positivity, e.g. positive messages in your diary, on your fridge and on the wall. Watch comedies.

5. Socialise with positive people.

"While I was planting some bulbs today,
I dug up an ancient civilization."

Other Serotonin Producers

1. Enjoy bright sunlight.

2. Eat a healthy diet with fresh vegetables and oily fish.

3. Have a massage.

4. Laugh. Watch funny films and series, read funny books and enjoy time with your friends.

5. Help someone out. Give them your time, help, money, cakes, etc.

"I have just initiated your computer's auto destruct countdown."

Why Am I Self-Destructive?

1. Your primitive mind keeps you alive. It relies on the information that is stored in your filing cabinet. If you had a cigarette after a stressful day and you survived, your primitive mind will encourage you to smoke as it did not kill you. It does not like change.

2. You need to think with your intellectual brain which knows that smoking is bad for your health.

3. Surround yourself with positive messages so they are stored in your filing cabinet as the truth.

4. Before you do something self-destructive, stop, pause, take deep breaths and smile.

5. The pre-frontal cortex, the boss in your brain, is in control. Put your trust in it.

"To maximize your wellness, we're going to work out for two hours every day!"

Exercise

1. Exercise fights depression, anxiety and anger so get moving.

2. Exercise reduces the effects of stress.

3. Exercise improves your brain's executive function and helps the boss in your brain do a good job.

4. It boosts brain-building hormones.

5. It stimulates brain growth, even with older people.

"Tell me this isn't celery."

Brain Food

1. The brain itself is 80% water so make sure you drink enough on a daily basis. If not, it can cause symptoms like brain fog, fatigue, dizziness, confusion and brain shrinkage.

2. Coffee and green tea is beneficial for the brain.

3. Eat oily fish such as salmon, tuna and sardines once a week and white fish once a week.

4. Eat complex carbohydrates (brown rice and bread), blueberries, turmeric, broccoli, pumpkin seeds, dark chocolate, nuts, oranges and eggs.

5. Be careful when you eat white pasta and bread, cakes, biscuits, ready-made and processed food. Alcohol is bad for mental health as it reduces the production of serotonin.

"Just look cute. Then we'll take over the household."

Touch

1. Physical contact is vital for our mental and physical health.

2. Hugs are massive stress busters. Join a hug class, hug club or give someone a hug.

3. Loneliness has severe consequences. It can cause mental health problems, heart disease and a shorter life span.

4. Any kind of physical contact is beneficial so book a massage and pamper yourself.

5. Adopt a pet or borrow someone else's. Go to a farm or a cat café.

"Let me know if I'm distracting you."

Music

1. Music improves your mood and reduces stress.

2. Music makes you more productive and creative.

3. Music acts as a natural remedy and reduces the symptoms of mental disorders.

4. Music affects each brain differently.

5. Your brain and body synchronise with the beats and rhythm of the music so listen to upbeat, happy music during the day and slow, relaxing music before you go to bed.

"I need someone inside the financial jungle."

Nature

1. Being in nature allows the pre-frontal cortex, the boss in your brain, to rest and recover.

2. Living near green space is good for your mental health, even if you do not use it.

3. Have photos and pictures of nature at home and in your work place.

4. Get out and about and you will better.

5. Watch YouTube clips of nature. They are very relaxing and make you feel content and calm.

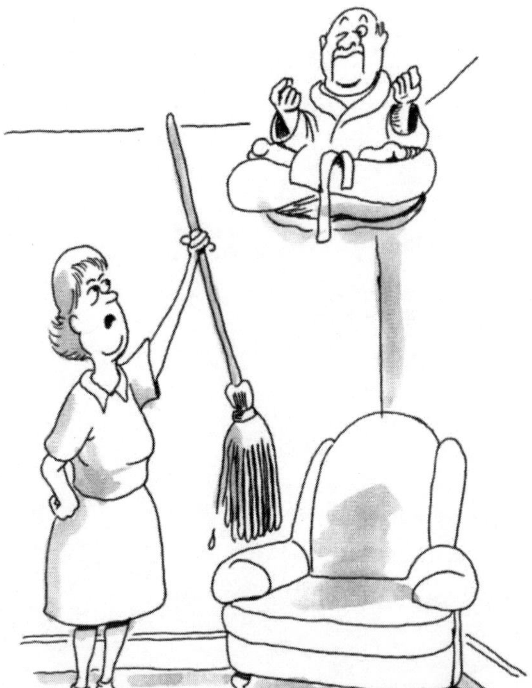

Meditation

1. Meditation is relaxing your brain and going into daydream mode. You can do this anywhere at any time.

2. Meditation is a great way to reduce anxiety and depression.

3. Meditation has been linked to larger amounts of grey matter in the brain which leads to more positive emotions and longer-lasting emotional stability.

4. Go to a meditation or yoga class. There are also many meditation lessons on YouTube.

5. Sit in a comfortable position, close your eyes, take deep breaths and imagine that you are in your perfect place without any worries.

"Okay, she's got her card in, now shut it down."

Laughter

1. Laughter boosts mood, protects you from the damaging effects of stress, strengthens your immune system and diminishes pain.

2. You do not feel anxious, angry or sad when you are laughing.

3. Laughter reduces stress hormones and increases energy.

4. Laughter allows you to see situations in a more realistic, less threatening light.

5. Laughter draws you closer to others and improves relationships, so get together and have a laugh.

"He is a Creature of the Web!
He must log on to survive!"

The Internet

1. Social media gives our brain the same dopamine hit as alcohol, drugs and gambling.

2. Many people are physically addicted to technology.

3. Many youngsters cannot create normal relationships without the internet.

4. Limit yourself to one or two hours per day and never at night. Your sleep is vital for good mental and physical health.

5. Join a club or organisation and meet new people.

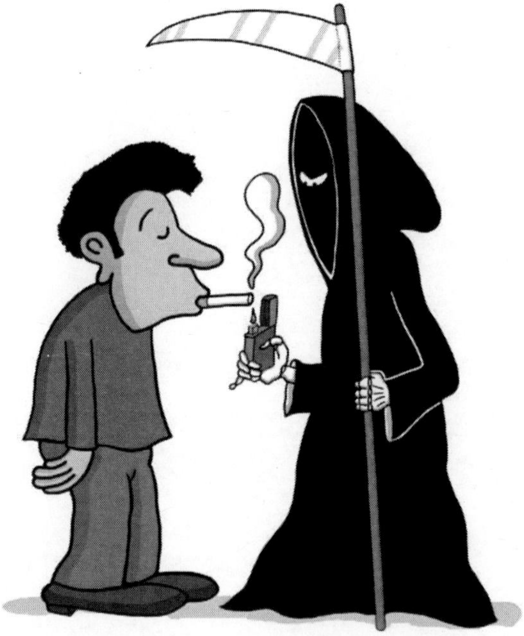

Smoking

1. When you inhale cigarette smoke, it affects the brain within ten seconds. It causes the release of adrenalin which increases heart rate and blood pressure and also restricts blood flow to the heart muscle.

2. Smoking reduces the production of serotonin, which regulates your general mood, by 50%.

3. Cigarette smoke is composed of more than 7000 toxic chemicals and tar.

4. Stop smoking now.

5. Help others to stop smoking. It affects everyone in their vicinity.

"We've got some hot new drugs for the summer season."

Drugs

1. Drugs interfere with the way neurons send, receive and process signals via neurotransmitters. They have a massive impact on your mental health.

2. A drug user eventually feels flat, lifeless, depressed and without motivation. They have problems enjoying normal life.

3. Do not use drugs.

4. If you use drugs, join a support group to help you stop. Your doctor can help you find one.

5. Talk to your family and friends about how you feel and ask them for help.

"Are you sure you tried hard enough to be on time?"

Why Do Others Stress Me Out?

1. A lot of stress is caused by personality clashes.

2. A person's personality refers to "the way they are most often".

3. We are born with our personality which can be found in the frontal area of our brain.

4. William Marston's personality theory categorises four types of people: dominant (D), influential (I), steady (S) and compliant (C). We have a mix of these four types in us.

5. Do the free DISC personality test to find out what DISC mix you are and tips on how to deal with the other personalities.

   www.123test.com/disc-personality-test/

"My last comment 'appeared' to be inviting feedback.
Do not be fooled."

Dominant Type

1. They enjoy dealing with problems and challenges. They are demanding, forceful, egocentric, strong willed, determined, aggressive and ambitious.

2. They are often leaders although their weaknesses include being poor listeners, impatient and insensitive to others.

3. Status is very important to D type people.

4. Show them how they can succeed and how they might fail. That is how you get listened to.

5. High D type people are prone to anger as their primitive brain's opt out clause.

"Are you in the mood to be amazed?"

Influential Type

1. They influence others through talking and activity. They tend to be emotional. They are enthusiastic, magnetic, persuasive, warm, trusting and optimistic.

2. They like people and thrive in a social scene. They are more interested in people than in accomplishing tasks.

3. They are excellent at communication, sales and marketing.

4. Be friendly and motivate them to finish tasks.

5. High I type people can be very dramatic and can move from depression to anxiety, anger and happiness at a fast rate.

"My profession has probably been transformed again just since we started this session."

Steady Type

1. They do not like sudden change. They like a steady pace and security. They are calm, relaxed, patient, predictable, stable and consistent.

2. They are the helpers in the world, e.g. doctors, nurses and teachers.

3. They do a lot of hard work in the background and are not often noticed as they do not like the limelight.

4. Recognise and appreciate their achievements. Give them time to adjust to change and avoid hurry and pressure.

5. High S type people are prone to depression as their primitive brain's opt out clause.

"There is no getting away from you guys."

Compliant Type

1. They adhere to rules, regulations and structure. They like to do things well and are slow-paced and task-oriented.

2. They are careful, cautious, neat, systematic and accurate.

3. They like technical jobs, e.g. engineering, auditing, accounting, etc.

4. Be patient, persistent and diplomatic as they are not good with people and communication.

5. High C type people are prone to anxiety as their primitive brain's opt out clause.

"The announcement of the changes really went well."

Why Can't I Change?

1. Prosci's ADKAR model tells you why you cannot change and how you can help yourself and others.

2. ADKAR stands for Awareness, Desire, Knowledge, Ability and Reinforcement.

3. Think of a change and score yourself out of 5 for the following: Do you have enough information about the change? Do you want to change? Do you know how to change? Do you have a support network to help you change? Is there reinforcement (regular check-ups)?

4. Look at the areas where you score 3 and below and focus on those. Ignore the others.

5. Your doctor can suggest help groups for mental health, weight loss, smoking, addictions, etc.

"People were quite receptive to the Change Seminar."

Dealing With Big Changes and Loss

1. When people are faced with big changes and loss, they all go through the same emotions.

2. The Kubler-Ross change curve shows that people go through the following stages: denial, anger, bargaining, depression, acceptance and moving on.

3. People move through these stages at different speeds.

4. Your history, personality type and the type of change are key factors in how you are going to respond.

5. If you need help going through the stages, see your doctor who can refer you to specialists.

"Of course I'm not mad.
What makes you think I'm mad?!"

Mental Health Disorders

1. Mental health disorders refer to a wide range of mental health conditions that affect your mood, thinking and behaviour.

2. Examples of mental illness include depression, anxiety disorders, schizophrenia, eating disorders and addictive behaviour.

3. If you think you suffer from a mental health disorder, consult your doctor. In most cases symptoms can be managed with a combination of medication and talk therapy.

4. Solution focused therapy concentrates on finding solutions for the future instead of analysing the past.

5. Find yourself a therapist who keeps up to date with science.

He had reduced his business strategy
panic attacks to under three hours.

Burnout

1. Burnout is a state of emotional, physical and mental exhaustion caused by excessive and prolonged stress.

2. You experience a burnout when your stress bucket has been overflowing for a long period of time.

3. Burnout is very serious and you should seek professional help immediately as you have damaged your health.

4. Your doctor will prescribe time off so you can recover. Take it easy and build up your physical and mental strength. This can take many months.

5. Reach out to those closest to you and seek social contact.

WE GOT YOU A PRIVATE NURSE IN THE OFFICE. SO YOU DON'T NEED TO STAY IN HOSPITAL.

Pain

1. Aches and pains can result from increased levels of stress. The stress hormone cortisol is associated with chronic pain.

2. Pain and illnesses can cause stress because you might worry about your job and money. You might be off work and alone in the house, resulting in loneliness.

3. Make sure you have eight hours of sleep because it heals your body and empties your stress bucket.

4. Do things you enjoy, look for social contact and think positively. That way you produce a steady flow of serotonin which can block pain.

5. Meditate as you cannot feel pain when you are in a trance.

"Alright, I'll okay a personal day."

Suicide

1. Some suicide attempts are cries for help, especially if there are obvious signs and warnings. A doctor should be consulted immediately.

2. Mental health disorders and substance abuse are risk factors.

3. Contact the Suicide Prevention Team. Text "shout" to 85258 or phone the Samaritans on 116 123 for free in the UK. Your doctor can also help.

4. Many factors were involved in making the decision to commit suicide so do not put the full blame on yourself.

5. There are local support groups for those who are left behind (uksobs.org in the UK).

"Stop yelling 'bingo' every time you get a bite."

Happiness

1. Happiness means many things to many people depending on age, gender and personality.

2. Dominant personality type people love status and expensive items. Influencers love travelling, fun and freedom. Steady type people like stability, safety and a comfortable home. Compliant type people love gadgets and new technology.

3. Do not focus too hard on achieving "happiness". Relax and enjoy the ride.

4. Stop and pause. Observe the here and now. You find happiness in small things.

5. Beauty and happiness is in the eye of the beholder.

"Happy Hump Day."

Creating Better Relationships

1. You can create better relationships and influence others by mirroring.

2. When you mirror someone, you take on their body language and talk about the things they are interested in. Unconsciously you create a close bond and trust.

3. Surround yourself with positive people and start mirroring them.

4. Let others mirror you. Smile and you will be smiled at in return.

5. Even a few minutes of mirroring improves relationships.

Whenever his boss praised him, he broke into the biggest smile.

Smile

1. The feel good neurotransmitters dopamine, endorphins and serotonin are released when you smile.

2. Smiling relaxes your body and lowers your heart rate and blood pressure.

3. Smiling makes you more attractive.

4. Smiling tricks your brain into feeling happy and healthy.

5. Smile and notice the positive reactions of others.

Wow, that is a really big goal!
I bet we can easily reach that goal
Let's work to exceed that goal!
What are we looking at?

Setting Goals

1. Your brain is programmed to achieve your goals, so it is important to take time out and think about your future.

2. Write down your goals. You are more likely to work towards them.

3. Tell someone what your goals are. It increases the likelihood that you will stick to them.

4. Divide your goals into smaller sub goals.

5. Celebrate! It feels amazing to have reached a goal.

Jack and Ina built their dream house.

Visualisation

1. Visualise your goals. Your brain is programmed to achieve them.

2. Visualisation can be as effective to improve skills as real practice. Coaches encourage their clients to visualise.

3. When you visualise an action, the same regions of the brain are stimulated as when we perform it and the same neural networks are created.

4. Close your eyes and imagine a goal. Make the scene as real as you can using your five senses. Make it vivid. Combine this with a strong positive emotion.

5. Repeat this procedure often, preferably daily. Your brain will start making decisions in order for you to achieve your goal.

"The quarterly results are in.
We would like to thank the almighty dollar."

Gratitude

1. People who practice gratitude by taking time to notice and reflect on the things they are thankful for, experience more positive emotions, feel more alive, sleep better and have stronger immune systems.

2. Gratitude is a great happiness booster and reduces stress.

3. Keep a gratitude diary. Regularly write brief reflections on what you are grateful for.

4. Thank people in person and make their day.

5. Write thank you cards, email and messages.

"It looks like you have everything under control."

Take Control

1. Your brain does not like unresolved issues. Take control and finish them.

2. You are in control of your destiny. The pre-frontal cortex, the boss in your brain, is in control and can overrule your primitive brain which causes depression, anxiety and anger.

3. Start taking control with small things. Before you go to bed, tidy up and wash the dishes. You will be surprised how good you feel.

4. Avoid multi-tasking. Finish one task before starting another one.

5. Believe in yourself and your brain.

"Thank you for gently guiding me toward insight."

Help!

1. If you feel you cannot cope, you should see a doctor who can refer you and possibly prescribe medication.

2. If you are in distress, need immediate help and are unable to see a doctor, you should visit the A&E department at your local hospital.

3. Talk to the Samaritans. They offer emotional support in full confidence 24 hours a day and the call to 116 123 is free in the UK.

4. There are many specialised support groups. Google what you are looking for and see how they can help.

5. Talk to friends and family about how you feel and surround yourself with positive people who can help.

Useful Websites

www.nhs.uk/oneyou

www.mind.org.uk

www.mentalhealth.org.uk

www.time-to-change.org.uk

www.rethink.org

www.supportline.org.uk

www.stem4.org.uk

www.papyrus-uk.org

www.youngminds.org.uk

www.thecalmzone.net

www.sane.org.uk

www.centreformentalhealth.org.uk

www.combatstress.org.uk

www.alcoholics-anonymous.org.uk

ukna.org

www.cruse.org.uk

More About BECS

About Us

BECS is an award-winning training company that has been based in London and the English Riviera since 2004. We deliver tailor-made solutions to the public and private sector. We help companies, schools, healthcare and government organisations get the best out of their people.

Our trainers and coaches have worked in a wide range of industries worldwide and offer real-life solutions and examples, not just theory. The courses and workshops are designed to be highly practical, interactive and fun. We share ideas, tools, tips, techniques and strategies and also provide follow-up coaching.

BECS Training and Coaching

- Business Skills
- Management Skills
- Mental Health Skills
- London Chamber of Commerce and Industry Qualifications

Why Choose BECS?

- Tailor-made solutions
- Small team of qualified and experienced trainers and coaches
- Up-to-date, interactive, multi-media training style
- Brain based learning
- Excellent feedback
- Choice of venues
- Competitive pricing

Venues

- In-Company Worldwide
- London
- Devon, SW England
- Kuwait
- Online One-to-One Sessions

www.becsltd.com

info@becsltd.com

Contact Details

BECS

126 Aldersgate Street

London

EC1A 4JQ

Tel. 0044 (0)203 3683441

Linkedin:www.linkedin.com/company/business-english-consulting-service-ltd/

Twitter: www.twitter.com/answinnen

Facebook: www.facebook.com/becs

www.becsltd.com

www.answinnen.com

info@becsltd.com